MW00716471

Bring Forth Hope

Pope Francis Speaks

to the Youth of the World

Christopher Ryan MGL

saint mary's press

The publishing team included John M. Vitek, editor; pre-
press and manufacturing coordinated by the production
departments of Saint Mary's Press.

5038

ISBN 978-1-59982-629-5

dedication

For Ella, Grace, James, Bonnie, Sarah, Paris, Allanah, and Isaac

It was an extraordinary moment, the evening of March 13, 2013! Thousands of people flooded Saint Peter's Square at the Vatican as the news spread that white smoke had been spotted from the chimney above the Sistine Chapel. A new pope had been elected! An extraordinary cheer erupted as Cardinal Jorge Mario Bergoglio, now Pope Francis, emerged from behind the curtain to greet the people gathered below, and to greet the world.

The square went silent as the Holy Father prepared to speak. In fact, the watching world seemed to be holding its breath, waiting to hear the first words of the new Pope. With a somewhat shy smile, Francis began, "Brothers and sisters, good evening," and the crowd erupted again. From that simple greeting, Pope Francis began an extraordinary conversation, a dialogue with the world.

In many ways, it has been an unusual conversation, at least for a Pope. Pope Francis has foregone much of the usual formalities traditionally associated with the papacy. He regularly gives "off the cuff" homilies rather than speaking at length from prepared texts. When he does have a prepared text, he frequently departs from it or abandons it altogether to speak from the heart and address the real-life issues he encounters among the people gathered. In these conversations, he reveals himself as a humble man of God who desires only one thing: that all people of good will come to know the love and friendship of Jesus.

The Pope's choice of name is significant. By recalling the great Saint Francis of Assisi, the Holy Father has chosen to give witness to a Church that turns outward, especially to the poor, the suffering, and those alienated in any way. He is a simple man. After becoming Pope, he rang up his newsagent in Buenos Aires to cancel his paper delivery for himself. He personally called a woman who found herself unexpectedly pregnant and abandoned by the father of the child. In the course of the phone conversation, Pope Francis offered to baptize the baby. When journalist and nonbeliever Eugenio Scalfari wrote two editorials posing questions that he would like to ask the Pope, Pope Francis replied with a personal letter that was published in the newspaper; he didn't have someone else reply on his behalf. It is clear that Pope Francis wants to listen to people personally and then respond directly to them. He especially wants to connect with those who are on the edge of the Church, with those who don't believe, and with those who are hurting in some way.

Pope Francis particularly wants to speak with and listen to the young people of the world. In fact, he has done so on several occasions already. Without doubt, the most memorable conversations with young people so far took place at World Youth Day in Rio de Janeiro in July 2013. In a very real sense, Pope Francis's addresses at World Youth Day express the most important things he wants to say to the youth of the world. However, his pilgrimage to Rio is not the only time Francis has engaged in an explicit dialogue with young people. He has frequently taken other opportunities to speak with young people in homilies, in question-and-answer sessions, and in his weekly general audiences and Angelus addresses. Young people are dear to the heart of the Holy Father!

In this collection of fifty-two quotes of the Holy Father, you have the opportunity to explore themes that are central to Pope Francis's vision of what it means to be a Christian. Above all else, the Holy Father wants young people to encounter Jesus Christ. He wants you to experience the love that God has for you. He wants you to know that you have been forgiven through the death of Jesus, and he wants you to know the joy that comes from the discovery that Jesus is risen from the dead! Pope Francis also challenges you to live a life that matters. He wants you to generously serve others, especially the poor. He wants you to be at the forefront of a Church that is going out to care for those who are hurting, forgotten, marginalized. The Holy Father wants to inspire and encourage you. He believes you are capable of great things for God and for others!

The book you are now holding in your hands continues the conversation the Pope has begun with the youth of the world. You might like to think of it as Francis's personal conversation with you. There are fifty-two reflections, one for each week of the year. Each reflection begins with a short quote from the Holy Father to young people.

Think About That

After each quote from the Holy Father, you are invited to reflect further on his words in the "Think About That" section. In a way, this section invites you to listen deeply to Pope Francis and to take his words to heart. The Holy Father often urges us to "listen for the answer in the silence of our own heart." This is where the Spirit is at work—in the silence of our reflective heart.

Take Action

The last thing Pope Francis would want is for you to merely listen to his words and not put your faith into action. In the "Take Action" section, you will find a suggested action that may invite you to pray, to write down your reflections and responses, or to read a passage of Scripture. You will also be invited to do something practical and concrete for others, because we are all called to love others as we have been loved by Jesus. In this way, Pope Francis asks you to express your love for God in deeds and not just words.

Say a Prayer

Pope Francis's conversation with you is intended to be the launching pad for a conversation with the Lord Jesus. The Holy Father wants you to pray, to enter into a dialogue with God. You can use the prayer that has been provided each day of the week as the springboard for your personal conversation with God. The line from Scripture at the top of each reflection can also help lead you into prayer. I invite you also to turn to Scripture each week and read the Word of God as a source that feeds your spiritual life.

A simple refrain runs through these reflections from Pope Francis: the Holy Father calls you to "put on faith," to "put on hope," and to "put on love." In a characteristically earthy image, Pope Francis explains that "putting on faith" is like adding salt or oil to a plate of food. The salt or oil does not remain on the surface of the food but rather changes the flavor of the whole meal. In the same way, when you "put on faith, hope, and love," when you "put on Christ," your whole life is changed.

May you enjoy this conversation with Pope Francis, and may his words lead you to a life-changing encounter with Jesus Christ!

Fr. Chris Ryan MGL

You will show me the path to life, / abounding joy in your presence.

—Ps 16:11

" Put on faith, and life will take on a new flavor, life will have a compass to show you the way."

—Pope Francis, World Youth Day 2013, welcoming ceremony

Think About That

The Holy Father offers two striking images to tell us about the difference faith makes in our life. Like salt, faith gives flavor to every part of life. Every aspect of our life is richer, fuller, and deeper in friendship with Jesus Christ. Like a compass that indicates the right way for a traveler, faith also provides direction to our life. When we have faith, we can trust in a path for our life. Through these images, the Holy Father is saying that faith changes everything. It makes the ultimate difference in our life.

Take Action

It might sound obvious, but have you ever asked God for faith? Take some time in silence to write a prayer in your journal asking the Lord for the kind of faith that "flavors" every part of your life and gives you a sense of purpose and direction.

Say a Prayer

Lord Jesus, increase my faith! I want my faith in you to bring meaning and fulfillment to my life. I want my faith in you to flavor every part of my life. Friendship with you changes everything.

My sheep hear my voice; I know them, and they follow me.

—Jn 10:27

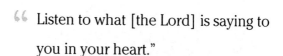

" Listen to what [the Lord] is saying to you in your heart."

—Pope Francis, World Youth Day 2013, vigil

Think About That

Our heart is the special place where the Lord dwells and speaks to us personally, where the Lord speaks to the deepest part of us. When we take the time to be silent and listen to the Lord in our heart, we discover that he has the words we really need.

Take Action

It is not always easy to listen to Jesus, because our mind and heart are often so noisy. Try to find some time each day this week to be silent so that you can hear the Lord speaking to you. Simply sit in silence and listen for what Jesus may have to speak to you.

Say a Prayer

Speak, Lord, your servant is listening. Help me hear what you are saying to me in the depths of my heart, and give me the courage to do what you ask.

I have told you this so that my joy might be in you
and your joy might be complete.

—Jn 15:11

Love

" If we are truly in love with Christ
and if we sense how much he loves
us, our heart will 'light up' with a joy
that spreads to everyone around us."

—Pope Francis, World Youth Day 2013,
homily at Aparecida, Brazil

Think About That

Joy is the greatest sign that a person has met
Jesus and fallen in love with him. It is the
happiness that comes from knowing that we
are loved by God, that we are loved personally, deeply, and intimately. The Holy Father
has shared with us this secret of true joy: It is
the result of knowing that Jesus loves us. Pope

Francis also says that this joy will spread naturally to those around us.

Take Action

This week, find the person in your class or at your workplace who is the most sad or lonely. Share your lunch with him or her. Just enjoy this person's company, and let him or her enjoy yours. Notice how this simple action can "light up" your heart and the heart of another.

Say a Prayer

Lord, I want my heart to "light up" with the joy of knowing that you love me, and that I love you. I want to spread your joy, especially to those who most need to know your love for them. Today I pray for those people I know who are sad and lonely. Make me a minister of your joy to them.

You take note of misery and sorrow; / you take the matter in hand. / To you the helpless can entrust their cause; / you are the defender of orphans.

—Ps 10:14

" We must never allow the throwaway culture to enter our hearts, because we are brothers and sisters. No one is disposable!"

—Pope Francis, World Youth Day 2013, address to the community of Varginha, Brazil

Think About That

Pope Francis is helping us to see that there are two fundamental ways of looking at another person: as a brother or sister, or as an object or thing. The second way involves a profound rejection of the dignity and worth of every human being. "No one is disposable!" This means everyone matters.

Take Action

Some individuals or groups do believe that others are disposable. They often want to eliminate the most vulnerable members of our society, such as the elderly, migrants or refugees, unborn babies, or those with a physical or intellectual disability. Take some time this week to visit someone who is homebound or sick, or someone who has recently arrived in our country.

Say a Prayer

Father, all of us are made in your image and likeness. We are all your children, so we are all brothers and sisters. Thank you for the dignity and worth of every human being. Help me see everyone I meet this week as my brother and sister.

Be merciful, just as [also] your Father is merciful.

—Lk 6:36

" The Cross of Christ invites us . . .
to look upon others with mercy and
tenderness, especially those who
suffer."

—Pope Francis, World Youth Day 2013,
Stations of the Cross

Think About That

People sometimes mock tenderness and mercy
when they see it. They regard these qualities
as signs of weakness. In fact, there is nothing
stronger than tenderness and mercy. They
are beautiful gifts that we can offer to others,
especially those who are suffering in some way.
Pope Francis is inviting us to be merciful and
tender to those who are suffering.

Take Action

Who is someone you know who is suffering in some way in this moment? What is the source of her or his suffering? What is one merciful word or tender action you can say or do for this person this week? Look to Jesus for the courage now to move beyond just thinking about saying or doing something—go to the person now and show her or him your mercy and tenderness.

Say a Prayer

Lord, you are tender and merciful to me. May others discover your mercy and tender love through me every day this week. Give me the courage to bring mercy and tenderness to another's suffering wherever I encounter it this week.

Your word is a lamp for my feet, / a light for my path.

—Ps 119:105

66 Dear young people: 'Put on Christ' in your lives. . . . Christ awaits you in his Word; listen carefully to him."

—Pope Francis, World Youth Day 2013,
welcoming ceremony

Think About That

The Bible is God's Word to us. It is a vital way to listen to him carefully. This means we can encounter Jesus when we prayerfully read the Scriptures, especially the Gospels. When Christ speaks to someone in the Gospels, he is also

speaking to us, to all people willing to listen, as
Pope Francis says, "with the heart."

Take Action

Spend 10 minutes each day this week reading
the Gospel of Mark in the Bible. When you read
a passage, ask Jesus what he is trying to tell you
about himself and his love for you and listen for
the answer in your heart. See if you can make
daily Scripture reading a habit in your life.

Say a Prayer

Lord Jesus, I want to know you more. I want to
encounter you in your Word. I believe that you
have the words of eternal life; help me listen.

But our citizenship is in heaven, and from it we also await a savior, the Lord Jesus Christ.

—Phil 3:20

66 It is the Resurrection that gives us the greatest hope, because it opens our lives and the life of the world to the eternal future of God, to full happiness."

—Pope Francis, general audience, April 3, 2013

Think About That

Many people live their life today as if this life is all there is. They live as if death is the end of everything. They have forgotten eternity. Jesus' Resurrection shows us that our life does not end in death. And so we can never forget that we are called to eternal happiness with God. We have an eternal destiny: we are created to be with God, not simply in this life, but forever.

Take Action

Many young people today are despairing because their life seems empty and alone. Find an encouraging quote about the importance of hope and post it on your Facebook page and your other social networks this week. Send it as a text message to your friends.

Say a Prayer

Lord Jesus, your Resurrection from the dead tells us that we are made for eternity with you. Help me remember that you have an eternal plan for my life. Help me make decisions today in light of eternal life with you.

Do you not know that the runners in the stadium all run in the race, but only one wins the prize? Run so as to win.

—1 Cor 9:24

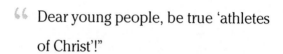

66 Dear young people, be true 'athletes of Christ'!"

—Pope Francis, World Youth Day 2013, vigil

Think About That

Athletes have to train hard if they want to win. Often they do some cross-training in order to build their strength and endurance. As Christians we need to train too! Our "cross-training" program includes prayer, the Eucharist, learning more about our faith, the guidance of wise leaders, and the service of others. Remember that we are also part of a team: the Church. Training with others is easier than training alone!

Take Action

How good are you at "cross-training"? Perhaps you are stronger at some parts of the training program than others. Can you identify your strengths and your weaknesses? This week, choose a part of the training program that you want to grow in and then commit 10 minutes each day to that activity, such as daily prayer, Bible study, or visiting with your youth minister or campus minister.

Say a Prayer

Lord Jesus, I want to win the "prize" you offer me—a happy, fruitful life, and being with you forever.

I even consider everything as a loss because of the supreme good of knowing Christ Jesus my Lord.

—Phil 3:8

" Faith immerses us in [Jesus'] love and gives us security, strength, and hope. Seemingly, nothing has changed; yet, in the depths of our being, everything is different."

—Pope Francis, World Youth Day 2013, welcoming ceremony

Think About That

What a wonderful description of coming to faith in Christ! We still look the same and sound the same, but in reality, "everything is different." Why? Because we have fallen in love—with Jesus. Everything seems the same, and yet everything has changed because we have met Jesus Christ.

Take Action

Can you point to a moment in which you felt immersed in Jesus' love? Did it bring a sense of security and strength as the Pope suggests? This week, reflect on that experience by writing it down in your prayer journal. When a person falls in love, he or she wants to tell others about it. This week, share with a friend why your faith is so important to you.

Say a Prayer

Lord, thank you for your love, security, hope, and strength. I believe you are changing me from within. Everything is different because I have met you.

Let us love not in word or speech but in deed and truth.

—1 Jn 3:18

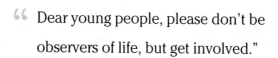

" Dear young people, please don't be observers of life, but get involved."

—Pope Francis, World Youth Day 2013, vigil

Think About That

Faced with so many choices in life, we can easily decide to sit on the sidelines and be spectators. Yet the Holy Father is saying that we won't find true life by holding back. We should not be afraid to be generous when Jesus asks us to get involved. We should not withdraw when we see someone in need of help or encouragement. We can easily think that it's best to keep our options open, but if we do that all the time, we will never commit to anything worthwhile.

Take Action

This week, don't sit on the sidelines. Pay attention and observe when you see someone in need, whether at your school, parish, workplace, or youth group. Reach out to that person, get involved somehow. Lend a hand or offer a listening ear.

Say a Prayer

Lord, give me the courage to wholeheartedly choose you and your life for me. Help me love richly and deeply, because I do not want to hold back.

Jesus, looking at him, loved him.

—Mk 10:21

66 We think we have to pray and talk,
talk, talk. . . . No! Let the Lord
look at you. When he looks at us,
he gives us strength and helps us to
bear witness to him."

—Pope Francis, vigil of Pentecost 2013

Think About That

Have you ever noticed that when a person is
nervous, he or she will often talk just to fill the
silence? We can do that when we try to pray.

Pope Francis tells us to simply let the Lord look at us. It is not always easy to hold the gaze of the Lord because his look of love is so complete and total, even overwhelming.

Take Action

Find an icon or a picture of Jesus, and place it in front of you. Let the icon be an aid to your prayer by reminding you that Jesus is looking at you. Quietly sit before the icon and simply look at Jesus. Don't try to say too much; just return his gaze of love.

Say a Prayer

Lord Jesus, lead me into silence. I'm not going to try too hard or say too much. I'm just going to let you look at me with love. Thank you.

Be kind to one another, compassionate, forgiving one another as God has forgiven you in Christ.

—Eph 4:32

" Dear friends, let us bring to Christ's Cross our joys, our sufferings, and our failures. There we will find a Heart that is open to us and understands us, forgives us, loves us, and calls us to bear this love in our lives."

—Pope Francis, World Youth Day 2013,
Stations of the Cross

Think About That

Isn't it a beautiful thing to be understood? It is amazing when we share something important with someone else and she or he really listens to us. We feel accepted, known, loved. Pope Francis tells us that Jesus truly understands us. This means we can share anything and everything with him.

Take Action

One of the greatest hardships in life is when we feel misunderstood. It can be a terribly lonely feeling. Is there someone in your life right now who feels you don't understand him or her? This week, invite that person to get together to talk with you. Use this time as a way to open your heart to each other and ask each other for forgiveness if you need to.

Say a Prayer

Jesus, you understand me completely. Give me the ability to listen to others compassionately so that they feel understood too. And when misunderstandings arise, help me to ask for forgiveness.

Go, therefore, and make disciples of all nations,
baptizing them in the name of the Father, and of
the Son, and of the holy Spirit.

—Mt 28:19

" I want you to make yourselves
heard. . . . I want the noise to go
out, I want the Church to go out
onto the streets, I want us to resist
everything worldly, everything
static, everything comfortable
. . . everything that might make us
closed in on ourselves."

—Pope Francis, speaking to Argentine youth, 2013

Think About That

Pope Francis knows that young people shake
things up sometimes. He thinks that's a good
thing! He wants you to stir things up as you

go out and proclaim the Gospel. The Good News of Jesus is not something we can keep to ourselves. Pope Francis wants you to lead the way: to be a bold witness to Jesus Christ! You may prefer to stay within the safe boundaries of your parish or youth group, but the Holy Father wants you to get out of your comfort zone.

Take Action

Will you be bold enough to share your faith with someone this week? At least once this week, see if you can "go out onto the streets" and in some way—in word or in action—give witness to your faith. What will you do?

Say a Prayer

Jesus, I'm not afraid to make some noise for you. I want people to know the life and freedom you bring. I want them to know the difference you make. Give me the courage to step out in faith.

Behold, I stand at the door and knock. If anyone hears my voice and opens the door, [then] I will enter his house and dine with him.

—Rev 3:20

66 This is how your faith grows—through encounter with a Person, through encounter with the Lord. . . . What is important is our encounter with Jesus, our encounter with him, and this is what gives you faith because he is the one who gives it to you!"

—Pope Francis, vigil of Pentecost 2013

Think About That

Pope Francis uses the word *encounter* four times in two sentences! He wants to make it really clear that the heart of our faith is an encounter with Jesus. The core of Christianity is meeting the Lord, knowing him personally, and falling in love with him. The Holy Father really wants to make sure we know this. More than that, he wants to make sure we encounter Jesus for ourselves!

Take Action

Sometimes our faith can seem weak or fragile to us. Pope Francis tells us that if we want our faith to grow, we should focus on our encounter with the Lord. This week, spend some time each day in prayer, telling Jesus that you want to encounter him more deeply.

Say a Prayer

Lord, the strength of my faith goes through all sorts of ups and downs. Sometimes I believe so strongly, and other times my faith feels really weak. I want to know you personally. Strengthen my faith through my encounters with you.

I am the light of the world. Whoever follows me
will not walk in darkness, but will have the light
of life.

—Jn 8:12

> " 'Put on hope' and every one of your
> days will be enlightened and your
> horizon will no longer be dark, but
> luminous."

—Pope Francis, World Youth Day 2013,
welcoming ceremony

Think About That

Luminous is a great word. It means "emitting
or radiating light." Pope Francis says that our
horizon will be luminous—full of hope, full of
light—if we "put on hope." It is important to
realize that we are not the source of the light.
The source of the light is Jesus. He is the Rising

Sun, and we radiate his light when we place our hope in him.

Take Action

It is not easy to hope when something or even everything seems to be going wrong. Sometimes life can seem dark. This week, get up early one morning while it is still dark and watch the sun rise. While you are watching, say the following prayer.

Say a Prayer

Lord, when everything seems dark and night has fallen, let me remember that the sun will always rise. When you feel a million miles away, help me remember that your coming is as certain as the dawn—that you are the source of light for my life.

Do not fear, for I have redeemed you; / I have called you by name: you are mine.

—Is 43:1

" Ask Jesus, speak to Jesus, and if you make a mistake in your life, if you should fall, if you should do something wrong, don't be afraid."

—Pope Francis, World Youth Day 2013, vigil

Think About That

We can often get very worried about making a mistake. It might be failing to fulfill our responsibilities at school or work, or letting someone down. We can be especially afraid of making a mistake when it comes to our faith. Sometimes this fear can paralyze us, but Pope Francis tells us we don't have to be afraid. He says that even if we do something wrong, we can always talk to Jesus about it.

Take Action

Failure is a normal part of the road to accomplishing something worthwhile or important. Our mistakes are often the launching pad for new ideas or ways of doing things. If you could be sure you wouldn't fail, what is one thing you would like to do for God or others? Make a start on it this week.

Say a Prayer

Lord, I'm scared of failing, of embarrassing myself. When I make mistakes, and even when I sin, help me learn from the experience so that I may grow into the person you want me to be.

He was made known to them in the breaking of the bread.

—Lk 24:35

66 'Put on Christ': he is waiting for you in the Eucharist, the sacrament of his presence and his sacrifice of life."

—Pope Francis, World Youth Day 2013, welcoming ceremony

Think About That

Jesus promised that he would never abandon us. In the Eucharist, he is really present to us. At the Eucharist, Jesus is with us in the most profound and complete way. There is no greater way in which we can encounter Christ.

Take Action

The Sunday Eucharist is an essential part of our life as Catholics. It is important that we go to Mass each Sunday because we need that encounter with Christ. We can also go to Mass on other days of the week if we are able to. This week, go to an extra Mass during the week and pay special attention to how the Lord is present to you in the Eucharist.

Say a Prayer

Lord, I believe you are truly present in the Eucharist. Help me encounter you in the Mass. I want to draw close to you and to share in your life.

I am the resurrection and the life; whoever believes in me, even if he dies, will live.

—Jn 11:25

" Let us feel the joy of being Christian! We believe in the Risen One who has conquered evil and death! . . . The Resurrection is our greatest certainty, it is our most precious treasure."

—Pope Francis, general audience, April 3, 2013

Think About That

Sometimes we think of Jesus as if he were just like any other historical figure: someone who belongs to the pages of the past. Or we think that he has returned to Heaven, which means he is still distant and remote from us. But the Resurrection of Jesus means that he is here with us now! It means he is always with us, close to us, present. Joy, incredible joy, is the result of this discovery.

Take Action

Every Easter we light a new candle as a symbol of the light and new life that the Risen Jesus brings. This week, go to a church and light your own candle to remind you that Jesus is risen from the dead!

Say a Prayer

Lord Jesus, I believe that you have risen from the dead. I want to know this, not just intellectually but at the deepest core of my being. As I light this candle, show me that you are alive and with me now.

While he was still a long way off, his father caught sight of him, and was filled with compassion.

—Lk 15:20

Love

" The Lord is waiting for us. . . . When we seek him, we discover he is waiting to welcome us, to offer us his love. And this fills your heart with such wonder that you can hardly believe it."

—Pope Francis, vigil of Pentecost 2013

Think About That

Lots of us like to try out new things, to experiment, and to go looking for new experiences. Did you ever think that when you do those things, it is actually God you are searching for? Pope Francis tells us the Lord is waiting for us in those moments, like the father who waited for his son to return home in Jesus' Parable of the Prodigal Son. When we receive the Lord's love and welcome, it seems almost too good to be true. Could he really love us that much? Yes, he does!

Take Action

This week, read the Parable of the Prodigal Son (Lk 15:11–32). How do you think the son felt when his father welcomed him home? Have you gone looking for new experiences recently? What does it mean to you that the Lord is waiting patiently for you, ready to welcome you home?

Say a Prayer

Lord, I don't always realize that I am searching for you. I know that sometimes I go looking for fun, excitement, and new experiences, thinking that is what I really need. Show me personally the truth of your love.

After laying the cross on [Simon], they made him carry it behind Jesus.

—Lk 23:26

" Jesus is looking at you now and is asking you: do you want to help me carry the Cross?"

—Pope Francis, World Youth Day 2013,
Stations of the Cross

Think About That

The Holy Father is thinking of Simon of Cyrene, who helped Jesus carry his cross to Calvary. In a mysterious way, we get to help Jesus carry his cross as Simon did. We do this by caring for those in need, by listening to those in pain, and by providing for those who do not have

enough. When we do this, we lighten Jesus'
burden and bring the love of Jesus to others.

Take Action

How are you being invited to help carry Jesus'
cross? Whose burden can you make lighter
by sharing his or her load? This week, make a
sacrifice of either time or money, sharing even
a little with someone in need in order to make
his or her burden easier.

Say a Prayer

Jesus, I love you and I'm willing to carry your
cross with you. Help me carry others' burdens
by sharing what I have with others.

For freedom Christ set us free; so stand firm and
do not submit again to the yoke of slavery.

—Gal 5:1

66 I know that you don't want to be
duple
duped by a false freedom, always
at the beck and call of momentary
fashions and fads. I know that you
are aiming high."

—Pope Francis, World Youth Day 2013, vigil

Think About That

Many things in our culture clamor for our
attention, and lots of things promise to make
us free. However, not everything that promises freedom actually delivers. Sometimes we
can be distracted by things that do not last or
that are ultimately unimportant. Pope Francis

believes in us though. He wants us to aim high. In fact, he doesn't want us to aim for anything less than God! He knows we can make good decisions about the things that really matter in our lives.

Take Action

This week, you might like to "fast" from an activity that can distract you from God. Turn off the TV and your phone for a little while each day and spend some time free of that distraction. You may be surprised by what you discover with this freedom.

Say a Prayer

Lord, we are often afraid to commit to things that matter or last. We are scared that if we do, we will no longer be free. Help us find true freedom by following you.

As each one has received a gift, use it to serve one another as good stewards of God's varied grace.

—1 Pt 4:10

" The Lord needs you, young people, for his Church. My friends, the Lord needs you!"

—Pope Francis, World Youth Day 2013, vigil

Think About That

Has it ever occurred to you that Jesus needs us? It might seem strange to think that God would need us, but the Holy Father reminds us that Jesus does need us to be his witnesses in the world. In fact, we are irreplaceable. No one else can do for Jesus what we can do for him.

Take Action

Take some time this week to write down a list of the talents you have been given by the Lord. Then select one of them to offer back to Jesus this week. Find one way to use one of your talents to make a difference in the Church and the world this week. What will you do?

Say a Prayer

Lord, you need me! I want to be your witness. Help me today to use the talents you have given me in the service of others.

With all my heart I seek you; / do not let me stray
from your commandments.

—Ps 119:10

" You like beauty, and when you

make music, produce theatre, and

paint—beautiful things—you are

looking for beauty, you are search-

ing for beauty."

—Pope Francis, August 28, 2013,
Diocese of Piacenza-Bobbio, Italy

Think About That

When we search for beauty, we are looking for
God, because God is all-beautiful. Pope Francis
wants to encourage us to create beautiful art,

because art reflects the beauty of the Creator. He also wants us to go to the source of all beauty: God.

Take Action

Take the time to visit an art gallery, see a play, or listen to some beautiful music this week. If you are an artist, create! Or watch the sun rise or set. Soak in the beauty, and let it lead you into an encounter with God.

Say a Prayer

Lord, you are the author of every beautiful thing. Let my search for beauty find its destination in you, for you are what I truly seek.

Then he poured water into a basin and began to
wash the disciples' feet.

—Jn 13:5

Love

66 Evangelizing means bearing personal witness to the love of God. . . . It
is serving by bending down to wash
the feet of our brothers and sisters,
as Jesus did."

—Pope Francis, World Youth Day 2013, final Mass

Think About That

We can get pretty anxious about sharing our
faith with others. It can seem so difficult and
scary. We must remember that it does not
depend on us, but on the Holy Spirit working
in us. Our life is changed by the Spirit, and we

find a new love emerging within us. Witness is simply allowing others to see and receive that new love.

Take Action

Is the Lord asking you to share your faith with someone this week? Find a practical way of showing that you love and care for that person. Don't be afraid to go beyond what is normal or expected. When you do this, you show the extravagant love of God.

Say a Prayer

Father, I want to be an instrument of your love today, this week, and always. Help me be the witness you call me to be. Spirit of Jesus, touch those that I serve this week through your presence and peace.

You have been told . . . / what the LORD requires of you: / Only to do justice and to love goodness, / and to walk humbly with your God.

—Mi 6:8

" [Young people], build a better world, a world of brothers and sisters, a world of justice, of love, of peace, of fraternity, of solidarity."

—Pope Francis, World Youth Day 2013, vigil

Think About That

The Holy Father challenges us not to be passive when we are faced with poverty, violence, and oppression of all kinds. He wants us to do something about it! It often seems like we are helpless when faced with overwhelming suffering and pain in others. Pope Francis reminds us that with Jesus' help we can make a difference.

Do you know someone suffering from injustice? Do you know someone in pain or deep loneliness? Are you affected by scenes of violence and poverty in other parts of the world? What is one practical thing you can do this week to build a better world? Now, do it!

Say a Prayer

Lord, I don't want to be passive when I see injustice, poverty, or hatred. Give me the courage to help rebuild the world according to your plans for us, a world of justice, love, peace, and solidarity.

As the first day of the week was dawning, Mary Magdalene and the other Mary came to see the tomb.

—Mt 28:1

" God does not choose according to human criteria. . . . The first witnesses of the Resurrection are women. This is beautiful. . . . Women have had and still have a special role in opening doors to the Lord."

—Pope Francis, general audience, April 3, 2013

Think About That

If the Resurrection of Jesus had been fabricated, then those inventing the story would not have chosen women to be witnesses, because testimony from women was not accepted at that time as legal evidence. Pope Francis suggests that this not only points to the authenticity of the women's story, it also means that women have a privileged place in proclaiming the Gospel. Women continue to be witnesses of the Resurrection all over the world today. Women continue to pass on the faith in homes, schools, parishes, and communities. Married women, single women, and consecrated sisters serve the Lord in all sorts of ministries in the Church.

Take Action

This week, take the time to thank some of the women in your life who show you the love of the Risen Lord through their words and example.

Say a Prayer

Jesus, thank you for the witness of the women in my life. Thank you for the way they have taught me about you, and shown me your love. Give them the courage and strength they need to continue to serve you and to share their faith with others.

They celebrate your abounding goodness / and joyfully sing of your justice.

—Ps 145:7

66 Dear young people, . . . I think of you crying out [Jesus'] name and expressing your joy at being with him! You have an important part in the celebration of faith! You bring us the joy of faith."

—Pope Francis, 2013 Palm Sunday homily

Think About That

Young people love to celebrate! The Holy Father is encouraging you to bring that sense of celebration, life, and joy to the Church. It belongs in the Church! You do not have to look elsewhere to express your joy or to celebrate. That's because the greatest reason any of us have to be joyful, and the best reason to celebrate, is Jesus, Emmanuel, God with us!

Take Action

The most important celebration for Catholics is the Eucharist. How can you "bring the joy of faith" to the celebration of Mass in your parish or community? Perhaps you can meet with your youth minister or parish priest and discuss ways the youth of your community can be invited into a more joyful expression of faith.

Say a Prayer

Lord, there is no one more exciting or wonderful than you. With you we have a thousand reasons to celebrate! Help me bring the joy of faith to others.

His mother said to the servers, "Do whatever he tells you."

—Jn 2:5

" So pray to Our Lady . . . and ask her, as a mother, to 'make me strong.' One thing that makes me strong every day is praying the Rosary to Our Lady."

—Pope Francis, vigil of Pentecost 2013

Think About That

An important part of our life of faith as Catholics is devotion to Mary, Jesus' mother and our mother. We can go to her and ask for her intercession when we feel like we need help. Pope Francis tells us that he asks for Mary's intercession to strengthen him on his journey. What would you like to ask Mary's help for in your own journey of faith?

Take Action

Take the time to pray the Rosary this week. As you pray each decade, ask Our Lady for something that you need to be able to be a better disciple of Jesus. If you need help in praying the Rosary, there are plenty of resources online. Don't forget to pray for the Pope too!

Say a Prayer

Mother Mary, thank you for your care and protection in my life. Help me do whatever Jesus tells me to do. I want God's will to be done in my life, just as you did when you first said yes to being the mother of Jesus.

Blessed are the peacemakers, / for they will be called children of God.

—Mt 5:9

Be anchored in this hope, the hope that comes from heaven! . . . You witnesses of Christ bring forth hope to this world that is aged by wars and sin! Go forward, young people!"

—Pope Francis, general audience, April 3, 2013

Think About That

The scars of war and sin litter human history, and they disfigure our world even now. The world is aged and weary from bloodshed and violence. Pope Francis tells us that young people are the hope of the world. If the world is ever to be free from war and violence, it will be because young people have brought the hope

and peace of the Risen Jesus to every conflict,
to every war zone.

Take Action

We can sometimes feel powerless when nations go to war with one another. It is important that we believe in the power of prayer and fasting in such times. We can also communicate to our leaders and tell them that they must find an alternative to war. We also need to be peacemakers closer to home. This week, spend one day fasting. Offer up your fast for the intention of world peace.

Say a Prayer

Lord, it is easy to become discouraged when I look at the destructive forces in the world. At these times, anchor me in hope, Lord! I believe that your peace will ultimately reign. Make me an instrument of your peace.

So, as you received Christ Jesus the Lord, walk in him, rooted in him and built upon him and established in the faith as you were taught.

—Col 2:6–7

66 Please do not water down your faith in Jesus Christ. We dilute fruit drinks . . . but please do not drink a diluted form of faith. . . . It is faith in the Son of God made man, who loved me and who died for me."

—Pope Francis, World Youth Day 2013,
speaking to Argentine youth

Think About That

Sometimes people try to tell us that faith is about being nice to one another or living by certain values. When they are asked about what it means to be a Christian, they leave out any reference to Jesus, and especially his death and Resurrection. Pope Francis tells us that this is diluted Christianity. We believe in Jesus, who loved us to death and who rose so that we might share in God's own life.

Take Action

Regular reading of Scripture, celebrating the Eucharist, and praying are the best ways to protect yourself against a diluted faith. You can also learn more about your faith. This week, see if you can attend a talk in your parish or a parish nearby to learn more about your faith.

Say a Prayer

Lord, I want to be your disciple. I don't want to water down my faith to make it easier. Teach me, and help me learn more about my faith from others.

He who did not spare his own Son but handed him over for us all, how will he not also give us everything else along with him?

—Rom 8:32

" The Cross contains all the love of God; there we find his immeasurable mercy."

—Pope Francis, World Youth Day 2013,
Stations of the Cross

Think About That

All the selfishness, violence, and darkness of the world is swallowed up by the love of Jesus on the cross. That includes your own selfishness and sin. On the cross, Jesus loves you at your worst, when you are least deserving of his love. His mercy has no limits; there is nothing he will not forgive.

Take Action

This week, take the time to look over your life and reflect on the good times and the bad times so far. Make sure you include those times when you or others were hurt by your actions. You could briefly describe each of those times in your journal. Then go back over what you have written, and write next to the good times, "Thank you for loving me here, Lord." Then, next to the times that describe hurtful actions or dark decisions, write "Thank you for LOVING me HERE, Lord."

Say a Prayer

Lord, when I look upon the cross, I see the lengths you go to in order to show me how much you love me. Thank you for your mercy!

Give honor to all, love the community.

—1 Pt 2:17

66 [We must] promote religious freedom for everyone, everyone! Every
man and every woman must be free
in his or her profession of religion."

—Pope Francis, vigil of Pentecost 2013

Think About That

In many parts of the world, Christians are not
free to publicly practice their faith, and are
even killed for doing so. People of other reli-
gions are also persecuted for their faith. Pope
Francis insists that none of these situations are
just. All people, regardless of their beliefs, must
be free to practice their own faith.

Take Action

Sometimes the challenges to religious freedom can be very subtle. This week, see if you can find examples of threats to religious freedom in our society or in another country. Write to your local political leaders about this situation, and ask them to advocate for these people whose rights are being violated.

Say a Prayer

Father, I pray for your children all over the world who are suffering today because of their beliefs. Give them strength and courage. I also pray for Church leaders, civil leaders, and lawmakers. May they protect the right to religious freedom for all their people, and not just those who share their beliefs.

I say to you, whatever you did for one of these least brothers of mine, you did for me.

—Mt 25:40

66 We cannot become starched Christians, those over-educated Christians who speak of theological matters as they calmly sip their tea. No! We must become courageous Christians and go in search of the people who are the very flesh of Christ."

—Pope Francis, vigil of Pentecost 2013

Think About That

These are strong words from the Holy Father! He is not denying the value of theology, but he is challenging us to put our faith into action! The people who are the very flesh of Christ are those who are poor. Jesus himself tells us that when we do something to the least of our brothers and sisters, we do it to him (Mt 25:40). The Holy Father wants us to give alms, to alleviate poverty by giving financially. But he also wants us to encounter those who are poor, to look them in the eye, to touch them.

Take Action

This week, volunteer some time in a shelter, at a soup kitchen, or doing some other activity that involves spending time with someone who is living in poverty. Go out, as the Holy Father says, "in search of the people who are the very flesh of Christ."

Say a Prayer

Jesus, you teach us that we meet you in those who are poor. Every encounter with you changes me. So change me, Jesus, as I seek to encounter you in my brothers and sisters.

Jesus saw a man named Matthew sitting at the customs post. He said to him, "Follow me." And he got up and followed him.

—Mt 9:9

66 [The Lord] is calling each of you to follow him in his Church and to be missionaries."

—Pope Francis, World Youth Day 2013, vigil

Think About That

It used to be that missionaries went to other countries to share the Gospel, but Pope Francis is saying to us that we are all called to be missionaries. To be a missionary simply means to share God's love with others. We are called by Jesus to be missionaries right now.

Take Action

There are lots of simple ways we can be Christ's missionaries in our everyday life. Think of someone you know who does not yet know the love of God. When you meet that person this week, take time to listen to him or her, and offer to say a prayer for him or her.

Say a Prayer

Jesus, being your missionary is not easy. I do want others to know that you love them and that you are the path to happiness, life, and joy. Help me share your love with others in gentle ways.

I have called you friends, because I have told you everything I have heard from my Father.

—Jn 15:15

" If we draw near to [Jesus], if we stay with him, what seems to be cold water, difficulty, sin, is changed into the new wine of friendship with him."

—Pope Francis, World Youth Day 2013,
homily at Aparecida, Brazil

Think About That

Some friendships can have the most unlikely beginnings. We can become great friends in unusual circumstances or after initial hesitations about whether we even like the other person. Pope Francis suggests that our friendship with Jesus often starts when we are finding things hard, or even when we have sinned. The Holy Father wants us to discover the extraordinary gift of friendship with Jesus. Jesus wants to be our friend!

Take Action

This week, spend some time each day talking to Jesus as you would a friend. Tell him what was good about your day, what was difficult. Share with him what has made you happy and what has been painful or sad. Don't forget to give him some time to speak to you as a friend too.

Say a Prayer

Lord Jesus, you want to be my friend! Thank you so much for wanting to be so close, Lord Jesus. I want to be your friend too.

As far as the east is from the west, / so far has he removed our sins from us.

—Ps 103:12

" 'Put on Christ': he awaits you in the sacrament of Penance, with his mercy he will cure all the wounds caused by sin. Do not be afraid to ask God's forgiveness. . . . God is pure mercy!"

—Pope Francis, World Youth Day 2013,
welcoming ceremony

Think About That

We don't like to think of ourselves as sinners. It means admitting that we have hurt someone else or ourselves. It also means admitting this to God, and we would rather pretend that everything is fine. Pope Francis tells us not to be afraid of repentance. When we confess our sins, we discover God's incredible mercy and love.

Take Action

Jesus is waiting for you in the Sacrament of Penance and Reconciliation. He wants to forgive you. Commit to receiving the Sacrament of Penance and Reconciliation this week, even if you have not done so in a very long time. See what you discover about the freedom and healing that come from God's mercy!

Say a Prayer

Lord, it is not easy for me to admit it when I do something wrong. I know I have hurt myself and others, and have therefore hurt you. Give me the courage to acknowledge my sins so that I might also know your mercy and forgiveness.

I have the strength for everything through him
who empowers me.

—Phil 4:13

66 Our own brothers and sisters [in
some parts of the world] . . . carry
their faith even to martyrdom. However, martyrdom is never a defeat;
martyrdom is the highest degree of
the witness we must give. We are
on the way to martyrdom, as small
martyrs: giving up this, doing that."

—Pope Francis, vigil of Pentecost 2013

Think About That

We often think of the early Church as the time
of the martyrs, but there are far more Christians
dying for their faith right now. We may not

be asked to die for our faith, but we can be ridiculed or rejected for what we believe. The witness of the martyrs who were willing to die for their faith can encourage us when others make fun of our beliefs.

Take Action

This week, research those people in other parts of the world who are being martyred for their faith in Christ today. Where do they live? Why are they being persecuted? What can be done? You might like to write a letter to your own political leaders or to human rights groups drawing attention to the suffering of our brothers and sisters.

Say a Prayer

Lord, give me the courage to be a witness. Help me to not be ashamed of my faith in you. When I am rejected and ridiculed for what I believe, help me respond with love and compassion rather than anger.

I live by faith in the Son of God who has loved me and given himself up for me.

—Gal 2:20

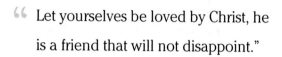

❝ Let yourselves be loved by Christ, he is a friend that will not disappoint.”

—Pope Francis, World Youth Day 2013,
welcoming ceremony

Think About That

It might sound strange, but it is not always easy to let ourselves be loved. Perhaps we have been hurt by someone we trusted, so it is not easy to let someone else love us. It can be especially difficult to let Jesus love us. We can be scared of what he might expect of us. But he is the perfect friend who will never let us down.

Take Action

Make a list of the qualities you most admire in a friend. They might include being loyal, compassionate, forgiving, generous, supportive, and many others. This week, let a friend or two of yours know what you most admire in them. Then see if all the qualities you wrote on your list apply to Jesus. He is the best of friends!

Say a Prayer

Lord Jesus, you want to be my best friend. Thank you for loving me, and help me let you love me more. I trust you, and I know you will not let me down. Help me be a friend to others in the way you model.

I, then, a prisoner for the Lord, urge you to live in a manner worthy of the call you have received.

—Eph 4:1

66 Dear young people, some of you may not yet know what you will do with your lives. Ask the Lord and he will show you the way."

—Pope Francis, World Youth Day 2013, meeting with volunteers

Think About That

When it comes to the future, young people are good at keeping the options open. There are so many possibilities. When it comes to your future, don't be afraid to ask Christ what he wants you to do with your life. We all have a particular calling to a unique vocation in this world. Jesus calls young people to different vocations—to the priesthood, to life as a consecrated sister or brother, to the single life, and to marriage.

Take Action

You may not have thought much about your vocation. Take the Pope's advice and ask the Lord what he wants you to do with your life. Take some time this week to meet with your youth minister, parish priest, or campus minister, and talk about different vocations in the Church and in the world.

Say a Prayer

Lord Jesus, I want to be open to your call. Show me what you want me to do with my life. I trust that the best place for me is where you want me to be.

Do not be conquered by evil but conquer evil with good.

—Rom 12:21

" Be the first to seek to bring good, do not grow accustomed to evil, but defeat it with good."

—Pope Francis, World Youth Day 2013, address to the community of Varginha, Brazil

Think About That

When we or someone we know is hurt by another, our first thought can be to retaliate or seek revenge. However, this only perpetuates the cycle of violence and hatred. The Holy Father points out that the true way forward is the way of Jesus: to repay evil with kindness and goodness. When we do this, we discover that love is the most powerful force on earth. Only love can bring the peace the world needs.

Take Action

Many young people today are bullied by others at school, at work, or online. Perhaps you or someone you know has been bullied recently. How can you care for these victims? This week, see if you can also talk to the bully. Help him or her see how people are affected by this behavior. Challenge the bully to treat others the way he or she would like to be treated.

Say a Prayer

Lord Jesus, you overcame evil with goodness when you forgave those who crucified you and when you rose from the dead. You showed us a way out of the cycle of hatred and revenge. Help me be an instrument of your love and peace.

So with old age is wisdom, / and with length of days understanding.

—Jb 12:12

66 Young people, salute [your] grand-

parents with great affection and

thank them for the ongoing witness

of their wisdom."

—Pope Francis, World Youth Day 2013, Angelus

Think About That

Do your grandparents play an important part in your life? Grandparents are usually great at loving us. They have often had an important role in teaching us about God and nurturing

our faith as well. Pope Francis tells us to thank
our grandparents for their wisdom.

Take Action

This week, take the time to thank your grandparents for their love, faith, generosity, and
inspiration. You might give them a call or visit
them in person.

Say a Prayer

Jesus, your grandparents, Saint Joachim and
Saint Anne, played an important part in your
life. Thank you for my grandparents and for all
they have given to their children and grandchil-
dren.

I command you: be strong and steadfast! Do not fear nor be dismayed, for the LORD, your God, is with you wherever you go.

—Jos 1:9

66 To embrace someone is not enough, however. We must hold the hand of the one in need . . . and we must say to him or her: you can get up, you can stand up."

—Pope Francis, World Youth Day 2013, Saint Francis Hospital

Think About That

Sometimes our friends find themselves in some sort of trouble. It may be a form of addiction or self-destructive behavior. Pope Francis encourages us not to sit idly by when someone is hurting themselves or others. He challenges us to put our faith into action by encouraging our friends to believe that they can change.

Take Action

Do you know someone who is caught in a self-destructive pattern in her or his life? You may not be able to fix the problem or change the person, but you can encourage the person to get the help she or he needs. Perhaps this week you can reach out to a friend, family member, or someone you know who is in need and offer her or him your support and encouragement. You can also pray for your friend.

Say a Prayer

Lord, I pray for all those who suffer from addiction or self-harm. I pray that they will discover your freedom, your healing, and your comfort.

For I know well the plans I have in mind for you
. . . plans for your welfare and not for woe, so as
to give you a future of hope.

—Jer 29:11

66 I repeat: never yield to discouragement, do not lose trust, do not allow
your hope to be extinguished."

—Pope Francis, World Youth Day 2013,
address to the community of Varginha, Brazil

Think About That

The ups and downs of life can provide all sorts
of challenges to our faith. Things don't go as we
had hoped, we get disappointed, and sometimes God seems a million miles away when we
feel that we need him most. Pope Francis tells
us that we have a choice in those moments. We
do not have to give in to discouragement and
lose our faith in God; we can decide to trust

and hope in Jesus, who is closer to us at those moments than at any other.

Take Action

Jesus promises us that he is with us always, especially when things are difficult or painful. How does this promise help you to be hopeful? How can you bring faith and trust to situations that are potentially discouraging or disappointing? You may wish to take some time each day this week to reflect on these questions and write in your journal.

Say a Prayer

Jesus, you are my hope. You are with me always, bringing light into the darkest moments of my life. I trust that you can bring life into every situation.

For those who are led by the Spirit of God are children of God.

—Rom 8:14

> 66 Let us think of God holding us by the hand. Then I would like to draw attention to this element: letting ourselves be led by him. This is more important than any calculation."

—Pope Francis, vigil of Pentecost 2013

Think About That

What a beautiful image! God is leading us by the hand. We often think that we have to forge our own path and find our own way, but as Christians we need to learn how to be led by the Lord. It takes faith and trust to let him lead us, but it is an essential part of being a disciple of Jesus. The Holy Father also tells us that being led by the Lord is an important part of sharing our faith with others.

Take Action

Programs are necessary, but they are only fruitful if the Lord is guiding our plans. Are you involved in efforts to reach out to others? If so, spend time this week getting involved in the effort. If not, this week find a program in your community that you can get involved with that reaches out to people in need. Commit to giving a little time each week to this effort.

Say a Prayer

Lord, I understand that it takes time to learn how you want to guide me. Help me to be patient and to not run ahead of you. Show me how to listen for your promptings and direction.

The one who sat on the throne said, "Behold, I make all things new."

" God always saves the best for us. But he asks us to let ourselves be surprised by his love, to accept his surprises. Let us trust God!"

—Pope Francis, World Youth Day 2013,
homily at Aparecida, Brazil

Think About That

Who could have predicted that God could love us so much?! He is always reminding us of his unfathomable love for us. When we know we are loved, we can do anything! This means that following Jesus is an adventure! He is always doing something new with us, something unexpected. If we let him, he will take us with him on a journey to places we never imagined or

could have dreamed were possible. Sometimes
we ignore the little promptings, the nudges
from the Holy Spirit that can open up surprising
new directions in our life.

Take Action

This week, if you feel a nudge to do something
for God that you have never done before,
give it a go! It might be volunteering for a job
or a ministry you have never done before. Or
maybe it's talking to someone about God. Step
out in trust!

Say a Prayer

Jesus, you are the God of surprises. I am filled
with wonder and awe when I realize just how
much you love me. Lord, I am ready for the
adventure! Guide me and surprise me. I'm open
to the unexpected, to the new things you want
to do with me.

The message of the cross is foolishness to those who are perishing, but to us who are being saved it is the power of God.

—1 Cor 1:18

❝ Dear brothers and sisters, no one can approach the Cross of Jesus without leaving something of himself or herself there."

—Pope Francis, World Youth Day 2013,
Stations of the Cross

Think About That

On the cross, Jesus takes upon himself our deepest fears, our loneliest moments, our greatest disappointments and sadness. He is with us even when everyone else seems to have abandoned us. This is precisely because he wants us to know that he is with us in the deepest darkness. We are never alone.

Take Action

This week, find a crucifix and hold it in your hands or touch it as you pray. What fears, shame, or suffering do you want to give to Jesus on the cross? What joys and hopes do you want to place before Jesus on the cross? Perhaps you might place a crucifix in your room as a constant reminder that Jesus is always near to receive your joys and hopes as well as your sufferings and sorrows.

Say a Prayer

Jesus, today I leave my *[fears, guilt, pain, joy]* with you on your cross. I believe you are with me, especially in those most painful and desperate moments. Thank you for bearing my burdens and receiving my joys.

All you who are thirsty, / come to the water! / You who have no money, / come, buy grain and eat.

—Is 55:1

"With our faith we must create a 'culture of encounter,' a culture of friendship . . . in which we can also speak with those who think differently, as well as those who hold other beliefs."

—Pope Francis, vigil of Pentecost 2013

Think About That

Often in the Gospels we read of people's encounters with Jesus, people who were from different ethnic groups, of different nationalities, and with different religious beliefs. In those encounters, Jesus became their friend. He invites us to do the same. Sometimes we can be suspicious of, frightened by, or intolerant of those who do not share our beliefs. Sometimes we can get into arguments when others challenge our beliefs. But something beautiful happens when we decide to become friends.

Take Action

You are probably already friends with someone who belongs to another religion or is from another culture. This week, take the time to ask that person more about what he or she believes. Let your friend ask you about your faith. Perhaps your friend does not believe in God at all. See if you can talk about what you both believe without getting into a divisive argument. Maybe you will both need to learn some more about your own beliefs so that you can tell each other more!

Say a Prayer

Lord, thank you for all of my friends. Thank you for those who share my faith in you and for those who believe in something else. Help me be a good friend to all of them. Help us respect one another and what we each believe.

I will fear no evil, for you are with me; / your rod
and your staff comfort me.

—Ps 23:4

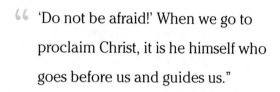

⁶⁶ 'Do not be afraid!' When we go to
proclaim Christ, it is he himself who
goes before us and guides us."

—Pope Francis, World Youth Day 2013, final Mass

Think About That

Pope Francis knows that our faith often feels
weak, and he wants to make sure it is not
destroyed by our fears. Sometimes we can be
worried that we will be rejected if we take our
faith seriously. We can also be scared of what
Jesus might ask us to do. The Holy Father tells
us that we have nothing to be afraid of if we are
with Jesus. God's love is greater than all of our
fears.

Take Action

It is important to face our fears. One way we can do this is by telling someone about them. This week, talk to your parents, your youth minister, or a spiritual mentor about what most scares you when it comes to following Jesus. Ask this person to pray with you for Jesus' strength to be with you.

Say a Prayer

Lord Jesus, again and again you tell us in the gospels not to be afraid. I believe you are stronger than all of my fears, and that with you I have nothing to be worried about. I give you my fears and anxieties, and in return I ask that you give me your peace.

Although you have not seen him you love him.

—1 Pt 1:8

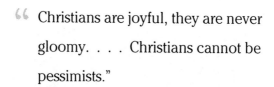

❝ Christians are joyful, they are never gloomy. . . . Christians cannot be pessimists.❞

—Pope Francis, World Youth Day 2013,
homily at Aparecida, Brazil

Think About That

What a challenge! Surely we have all met some very gloomy Christians. Pope Francis is saying that pessimism is deeply contradictory to the spirit of the gospels. When we know Jesus, we are filled with a joy that cannot be shaken, even by all sorts of trials and temptations. It is the joy that comes from knowing that Jesus is risen from the dead; he has conquered evil, sin, and death. This means that nothing need rob us of our joy.

Take Action

When we look at some of the terrible situations in the world, or in our own life sometimes, it seems easy to be pessimistic. At these moments, we need to see the situation from the Risen Jesus' point of view. Nothing is too great for him. What makes you feel gloomy from time to time? This week, consider ways in which you can get a new perspective on that situation. See if you can turn your pessimism into hopefulness about the situation.

Say a Prayer

Jesus, help me believe more deeply in your Resurrection. I know this means that goodness triumphs and that nothing is more powerful than your love. Never let me forget that you are risen! I want to share in the joy you experienced when you rose from the dead.

Some seed fell on good soil, and when it grew, it produced fruit a hundredfold.

—Lk 8:8

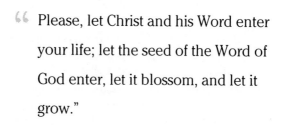

66 Please, let Christ and his Word enter your life; let the seed of the Word of God enter, let it blossom, and let it grow."

—Pope Francis, World Youth Day 2013, vigil

Think About That

Pope Francis reminds us of Jesus' parable that tells us that the Word of God is like a seed. The Holy Father is encouraging us to let Jesus' Word blossom and grow. If we are open and ready, the tiny seed of Christ's Word in us can burst forth in new and exciting ways. We're not always willing to let Christ's Word enter into our lives. Sometimes we can become numb, discouraged, or negative, and the Word of God gets stifled in our lives.

Take Action

Each day this week, take a few minutes to read Matthew 13:18–23 in your Bible. Reflect then on how you are providing "good soil" for Christ and his Word in your life.

Say a Prayer

Lord, I want your Word to grow in me. I know that it is the Word of life, the Word of love and Word of hope that I am searching for.

Once you were "no people" / but now you are
God's people; / you "had not received mercy" /
but now you have received mercy.

—1 Pt 2:10

" Jesus asks us to make his living
Church so large that it can hold all
of humanity, that it can be a home
for everyone!"

—Pope Francis, World Youth Day 2013, vigil

Think About That

Pope Francis believes the Church should be
big enough to accommodate everybody. That
sounds lovely, but in practice it's very challenging. It means welcoming those we find hard to
love and including those whom others have
rejected.

Take Action

Is there someone you find difficult to welcome to the parish, to your youth group, to your school? Do you know of someone that everyone else has excluded? This week, do something for that person to make him or her feel welcomed and at home. Show that person the hospitality of God by your words and your actions.

Say a Prayer

Jesus, you love everyone, and you want everyone to be at home in the Church. May all people discover their true home in you through your Church.

Put on the Lord Jesus Christ.

—Rom 13:14

" 'Put on Christ' and your life will be full of his love; it will be a fruitful life."

—Pope Francis, World Youth Day 2013,
welcoming ceremony

Think About That

We want our life to matter. We want others' lives to be enriched by our actions and influence. Pope Francis tells us that the secret to a fruitful life is living with Christ. If we "put on Christ," our life will be filled with his love—in fact it will overflow. And when Jesus' love overflows in our life, it will fill others with his love too.

Take Action

What sort of difference do you want to make? What is the great need in the world that you want to meet? What kind of legacy do you want to leave for others? This week, "dream" with God about your sense of a fruitful life. Talk to Jesus in prayer about your plans and hopes. You might also share your dreams with a close friend.

Say a Prayer

Christ Jesus, you are everything and you are in everything. I want to see you in everything I do, in everything that happens to me. Fill me with your love to the point of overflowing: I do not want to keep you to myself.

Index

Following each quote from Pope Francis is a citation that tells you where the quote comes from. You might like to find these documents so you can read the quotes in their original context.

2013 Palm Sunday homily. Palm Sunday homily, March 24, 2013.

August 28, 2013, Diocese of Piacenza-Bobbio, Italy. Dialogue with young people of the Diocese of Piacenza-Bobbio, Italy, August 28, 2013.

General audience, April 3, 2013. General audience in Rome, April 3, 2013.

Speaking to Argentine youth 2013. Meeting with the youth from Argentina in the Cathedral of San Sebastian. World Youth Day, Rio de Janeiro, July 25, 2013.

Vigil of Pentecost 2013. Address to new movements and communities at the vigil of Pentecost, Rome, May 18, 2013.

World Youth Day 2013, address to the community of Varginha, Brazil. Address to the community of Varginha, Brazil, World Youth Day, July 25, 2013.

World Youth Day 2013, Angelus. Address at Recital of the Angelus from the balcony of the Archbishop of Rio de Janeiro, World Youth Day, July 26, 2013.

World Youth Day 2013, final Mass. Mass for the 28th World Youth Day, Rio de Janeiro, July 28, 2013.

World Youth Day 2013, homily at Aparecida, Brazil. Homily for Mass in the Basilica of the Shrine of Our Lady of the Conception, Aparecida, Brazil, World Youth Day 2013.

World Youth Day 2013, meeting with volunteers. Meeting with the volunteers of the 28th World Youth Day, Rio de Janeiro, July 28, 2013.

World Youth Day 2013, Saint Francis Hospital. Visit to the Saint Francis of Assisi of the Providence of God Hospital, World Youth Day, Rio de Janeiro, July 24, 2013.

World Youth Day 2013, Stations of the Cross. Homily at Way of the Cross at Copacabana, Rio de Janeiro, World Youth Day, July 26, 2013.

World Youth Day 2013, vigil. Prayer Vigil with the young people, World Youth Day, Rio de Janeiro, July 27, 2013.

World Youth Day 2013, welcoming ceremony. Welcoming ceremony by the young people on the waterfront of Copacabana, Rio de Janeiro. World Youth Day, July 26, 2013.

Author Bio

Christopher Ryan is a Missionaries of God's Love (MGL) priest and is currently the rector of the MGL formation house in Melbourne, Australia. He is the author of *In the Light of the Cross: Reflections on the Australian Journey of the World Youth Day* (Australia: Saint Paul's Publications, 2009), a series of reflections on the Catholic faith from his pilgrimage throughout Australia with the World Youth Day Cross and Icon in 2008. Father Chris has been involved in youth ministry in parishes, schools, and new communities and is a popular speaker for youth and young adults.